CATALOGUING PAIN

Cataloguing Pain

Allison Blevins

 YESYES BOOKS *Portland, OR*

Cataloguing Pain © 2023 by Allison Blevins

Cover & Interior Design: Alban Fischer
Project Lead: KMA Sullivan

ISBN 978-1-936919-92-5
Printed in the United States of America

Published by YesYes Books
1631 NE Broadway St #121
Portland, OR 97232
yesyesbooks.com

KMA Sullivan, Publisher
Joanna Acevedo, Assistant Editor
Brandon Courtney, Senior Editor, Operations
Alban Fischer, Graphic Designer
A. Tony Jerome, Assistant Editor
Karah Kemmerly, Assistant Editor
Jill Kolongowski, Manuscript Copy Editor
James Sullivan, Assistant Editor, Audio Books
Gale Marie Thompson, Senior Editor, Book Development

For Taylor

Contents

I.

Cataloguing Pain as Marriage Counseling – 3
A Poem for When You Ask What's Wrong – 13
Fall Risk – 14
The Name in the Doorway – 16
A Catalogue of Repetitive Behaviors – 17
On a good night, we feel like talking. In our bed, I explain to my wife – 30
Diagnosis – 31
I can't forget how empty doorways stand, freezing – 35
How to Be Gay in Missouri – 36
Roadside bible verses – 37
Litany for the Living – 38
During the Days After My Official MS Diagnosis – 39
Blackest Black – 45
Pain as Memoir – 46
I can't forget, can't return, all the once – 47
Elegy for My Wife – 48

II.

This is the Only Conversation We Will Have About the Embryos – 53
Fly Season – 54
Pain as Caged Birds – 58
Daughter, before you thought in words – 68

3 am on the toilet, the shell forgets — 69
I know I'm still breathing from my lungs — 71
Running as Self-Portrait — 72
Everyone Waits at the DMV — 73
Cataloguing Pain as Non-Narcotic Pain Reliever — 74

Acknowledgments — 85

I.

Pain is frustrated that it is trapped in a body that is ill-fitting for its unfolded shape.
—SONYA HUBER

Cataloguing Pain as Marriage Counseling

When my legs slowly paralyzed—heavy rain, wood, stone—I spent hours holding tight to the kitchen table trying to lift each knee into the pressing air. An editor once asked in an encouraging rejection letter why the manuscript had to be so depressing.

My wife goes for a run, kisses me when she returns. I lick her salt from my bottom lip slowly as she showers, taste what it tastes like on the chin of movement and sun—pollen and residential trucks, all the retirees fertilizing impossibly green lawns—feel my lips *hello* to Clarence across the street.

You ask how I feel. This is a trap. If I say my body hurts, not in my skin or fascia but in the spreading of pain along my nerves from my mother to my daughters. If I say inside me pain learns something new: how to web into the small and wet, loiter in the old rooms of diving and blue. You will reply, *I'm sorry*. I'd rather argue.

Today is a bad day, but I dress anyway. Bra too. How many bra days do any of us have left? The children *ring-around* in the trampoline. One person in my online support group loses whole days, makes love and doesn't remember. What makes me Allison if it isn't walking or touching or these words and my memory of writing them?

In the closet we embrace. I'm hanging clothes half asleep. Flushing and chilled from drugs, I try to print the softness of the backs of your arms into my brain as they move against my forearms wrapped around you. The smell of your breath drifts into my open mouth pressed lightly to your neck. Thursday afternoon in August. I'm standing after a fall I will describe another day to my neurologist. Today there was blood.

Do you think of yourself as disabled? Do you think of me as a swallowtail, a fern, a dust-covered suit coat? She hates this. *No. You seem fine.* What do I know about living in a disabled body? *If that is how you really see yourself, you're lying to me about how much pain you feel.* This is when I should come out. I've forgotten how.

Last night I slept through our baby waking again. I'll never get her night-wakes back. My body hollows.

Today we argue, I imagine my wife young and weeping. She never cries. I've learned when to stop yelling—like so many men, her eyes rim red with water that never spills. I imagine how she smashed metal cars together as a child, fed her grandfather's cows, wore jeans thinned at the knees.

My wife says the word *flushing* is dainty as if I'm corseted with the vapors. *Do I feel hot when you touch me?* She is holding ice packs to my face and chest. *No.* Earlier I tried to explain the opposite of hunger but didn't mean full. I'm down eleven pounds. *Flushing* feels like fire—that isn't right—my veins are trying to escape from my pores.

I've been conscripted into an army of the unwell. We didn't know how pain waited beneath the surface of date night, lake weekends, weeknight prayers over chicken and rice. This is pain so green and real you suddenly feel so alive, not even birth makes a body this alive.

A Poem for When You Ask What's Wrong

Think of spring days—weather radio jolts you—
lemon poppy seed muffins, dishes, towels and whites.

By evening, grass still dry, sun slats through drooping
white pouches in gray-blue clouds and backyard greened limbs,

neighborhood children bike sidewalks, adults nod and wave.
We all know what roiling darkness passes just north of our stolen

evening, our cranberry and vodka, curb-scraped knees
and chiggered ankles. Think of my walking like this—

my steady step today as burgled. Imagine each morning I must open
my night-sleep closed wounds, choose between a spoon or scalpel.

Which would you prefer for the job? Imagine a billowing veil that never lifts
laced like stone into my hair. I'm not the dry asphalt, the retirees watering.

I'm not the clutched-kneed child. I'm the wailing
squall line, funneled wind—needle thrust out to waiting skin.

How many times each day must you consider pain? When you ask
what's wrong, imagine me as an opened animal twitching roadside.

Fall Risk

I.

After the fall, I call out for my wife. I can't cry. I can't feel pain now.
I call out for my wife, aware my breasts and belly hang like some white

unimaginable fruit—inedible and overripe. I call out because I can't rise
from my hands and knees until some witness lifts me on to my feet.

I won't cry or feel until she is here with her arms around me—shame
is the pain I was waiting for. Wet and drooping, *I've ruined sex night*,

I sob into her shoulder. When I hobble from the bathroom, she
is ordering a shower aid from the medical supply store.

II.

I want to fall, to watch your body bend, pick me up, feel your bicep
on my back, but you already cleaned the house today. I want to ask you

to touch me, but it is Wednesday—shot day—and you've already loaded
the injector, swiped in outward concentric circles, pinched my stretched

and marked skin between your thumb and forefinger.
I want to fall less in love with you.

No woman should have to expose herself to a lover's hands touching
like this, but desire vibrates from every greenblack circle on my body.

The Name in the Doorway

Our daughter waits in the doorway. She mouths *Mom* silently. My name floats from her mouth, hovers wordless above my body in bed. A blue and humming three-winged bird, my name waits and waits, lands softly on my mouth to wake my body from sleep, soft as the start of a pistol, soft as a lurching coaster, soft as a table leg in the dark. But our daughter is gone. Only the blurred and glowing outline of her body fills the doorframe. Maybe the stomach ached. Maybe the spider shadow crept. Maybe the water emptied. Maybe only my name left her pillow, flew across our house, dropped on top of me in bed. The name returns every night, every night to steal, every night to kiss my mouth.

A Catalogue of Repetitive Behaviors

I read articles about my new diagnosis: "signs of high-functioning autism in adults include repetitive behaviors, trouble reading social cues, robotic speaking patterns that don't communicate true feelings, invention of unusual descriptive words or phrases." My wife thinks this diagnosis should make me feel better. How do I explain lonely feels like lonely no matter what you name it?

Do you remember those girl nights? Soft, unburdened? You might run your hands slowly down your hilling body, girl-young you didn't yet know the ways a body could be dismantled. Here I do imagine us female.

Facial reconstruction. Tonsillectomy. Cervical biopsy. Arthroscopy. Bowel resection. Cold knife cone. Gland biopsy. Spinal tap. Gland removal. I try to keep hold of a running list of things that men who know better than me—my body—have done to my body.

I track pleasures through color and sound. When we wake the morning, our love is like an alarm blaring—pink-orange-morning-blues swirl and striate like cream in coffee. Love wakes the body like cologne lingers on the neck: this chair a proposal, this shirt a birthday surprise dinner, flashing lights and garbage truck rumble an awake-all-night kiss. When love wakes to love, these years crumble—divine and needing, needing to be kept, beautiful—*fuck*, what you and I have created: love wakes in my abdomen, in my teeth and blaring hair. We are not falling out but divers—headlong into a warming blue wonder.

Some days, I want to explain what birth has done to my body: each new ache, rash, crust of white lifting itself to upright on my skin. Today, it's my jaw. I tell myself, *give it two weeks.* Mostly the catalogue of ailments is stored, forgotten. I have trouble, lately, with the lie of it all.

In my accounting of scars, I want to name the deepest invisible rather than the raw and feathering at the edges, tight with glisten and pull. This scar is every time I pushed, blank faced, *nothing* against your reaching out then walking away. When I seem most not to want, that is the hunger—like a child reaching out her arms each night into a glowing, motherless dark.

My wife writes a letter to our son every year on his birthday. In the days after this diagnosis, the rhythm of footfalls and the running washer across our house keep me awake and safe. I hear the clocks' ticking in every room. I know the smell of her neck so well—*lift me from the bed, help me with the socks.*

I try to hold on to pleasure: the first time my wife's tongue inside me licked up toward my heart as if she had bit into an unexpectedly ripe fruit. Every day I think about leaving her for her own good.

Screams pile loosely in my throat and lungs like buttons. All of my children have one day choked: cracker, small plastic hair claw clip, pool water—trachea swelling to bark and stridor. Like blankets falling from tall shelves, some catastrophes paralyze me—large firework cannon tipped toward a crowd. Mothers know the full silence that lurks white and soft before sound erupts from a mouth.

Some nights, when we fuck, your elbow holding my arm down above my head bites too hard into the fleshy underside of my bicep—pain just deep enough makes me start to cry out *stop*, but I don't.

Time here moves fast and slow. I'm running toward a here without railings or my children to hold tightly by the shoulders. Here, inside, is a space that pushes toward a devouring center. Here is painful, not the empty but the filling whole swelling with gratitude. I'm so packed with gratitude I can barely stand or speak.

How to hang the head and make eye contact, how to apologize (not sorry), how to feel sorry, feel guilt, turn loathing to guilt, to anger, to guilt, how the organs have been hollowed from all our bodies, blood drained down a central system, how to carry it in the shoulders, how all the small cysts of guilt reside and remind us how to walk and lilt and what we should all be carrying.

Don't you remember the floor, the corner, and every night you promised to stop tomorrow, repeated the list in your head, whispered the words into your mouth. Today, your wife tells you, *Holding on is an addiction.* But you must number and track pain. Allison, your body is a shame you carry in the rapid whisper your tongue makes of one, two, three; how you keep the hurt, always lose the remember. *Lose* crowds out memories: the weight of your son in your arms, your daughters' fingers fat with sleep and wrapped to red around your finger.

On a good night, we feel like talking. In our bed, I explain to my wife

that when the Supreme Court heard oral arguments against gay marriage, my ex-wife had just abandoned the child she birthed. My daughter's chest fluttered each night in my bed like new leaves peeking from still-forming branches. When I stood in the yard and tilted my head back, I could smell the honeysuckle just beginning. All of this was tender. Think of how a petal oozes after it is crushed. Think of the liquid, gluey and coating the spirals. Then you are with me in that moment. Pain flashes now like a child's red plastic stereoscope. My pumping heart defines each moment as human, not like a metronome but a screen, maybe circular and revolving. And, yes, this is disorienting, this ever-spinning stage, all true as the tearing of birth, as the fresh green blood of something raw coming into a room for the first time.

Diagnosis

The neurologist called, *Your brain MRI showed another lesion.* Official multiple sclerosis diagnosis. I knew this was my moment to let go. I read the MRI report: T1 hypointense lesion. Called *black holes* in some medical journals. My paralysis, lesions, spinal tap—no longer historical like something I read about once in a now-shelved textbook.

Two weeks before the call, we decided to get pregnant again. We felt safe. Three embryos frozen and waiting. *You have to decide: pregnancy or try a new medication.* Does it make sense to say I lost a child the day we signed the fertility clinic papers?

The pain scale is no longer body or nerves: my locking hips, my tightening calf. Pain is memory. Pain is how my children used to run their bodies full speed into my body, the shush of an elliptical machine, that night we fucked on the living room floor of our first house.

Those who know better want me to measure, but pain finds new ways to pain. How to rate that the night cold now feels like wet drips on my legs and ankles, rate how somewhere in a New York clinic, three pieces of us have been tossed into an incinerator?

I can't forget how empty doorways stand, freezing

Wisconsin drops raining sleet under my collar,
how a navy sweater once held the bones
of a lover's neck—*Will you come back?*
Come back—how Missouri rivers would rise and rise to roadway,
scrub asphalt clean, how all the women in all my tangle-sheet beds—
I would have thrown my life away for you—shrank
and shrank to sinew, we were so high on Oregon sunsets,
all the losses, pennies twinkling on Iowa bedrock,
how, as a child, some of our gods promised and promised
sleep—*sleep child sleep*—darkness pulls
at the tight whiskering corners—but I can't blink away
every loss, every pain—toe, ankle, thigh—can't unsee,
unlove—*everything close enough almost to touch*—
all of those lovers' burned and electric outlines.

How to Be Gay in Missouri

Keep watch over your children. Forget about linger and loaf. Think of all the yeses you've spoken. Aim to be small. Remember loving the sound of some place: a hum or a whoosh. When the men come, when they swell, chests puffed full of gospeled breath, let them come. Be broken like kindling. Remember your mother's perfume. Think of the hills, deep and lasting. Keep watch over your feet. Slink into the cracks in the sidewalk. Be mud.

Roadside bible verses

line all the rural highways near your childhood home. I imagine you as a teenager parked on those gravel roads and all the girls, how you mouthed into their necks. I loved you the moment your mouth whispered into the soft skin behind my ear. I knew you'd done it before, practiced in the reclined seats of your red '94 Ford Escort—all the girls tilting toward your mouth and hands. Here I imagine you boy young and flushed with wanting.

Most nights you sleep with the covers pulled tight over your head. I think of the story your mother tells. How as a girl you carved your name into the piano, coffee table, kitchen cabinet. I want to wake you, pull back the covers, carve our pain into your body with my tongue.

Litany for the Living
for Karen and Georgia, hosts of the podcast My Favorite Murder

Corazon Amurao Rebecca Garde Kathy Kleiner Teresa Thornhill
          There will be no more death or mourning or crying or pain

Carol DaRonch
          I am fearfully and wonderfully made
Maria Viricheva
Whitney Bennett
Kate Moir
Gay Hardwick
    Even if I speak, my pain is not relieved
Tracy Edwards

    Terror will seize them, pain and anguish will grip them; they will writhe
Please imagine how it must feel, each day, for women, to live.

During the Days After My Official MS Diagnosis

You always need to discuss feelings, make plans. Yesterday, a man posted in your spouse's support group about his wife's dementia. [I wish you'd never told me.]

I'm wearing a white medical patch on my chest. Wires tickle between my breasts. I hoped you wouldn't notice our toddler pull the rectangular monitor from my pocket, pretend to phone her grandmother. She will never know me without a limp. The older two remember. This is joyful—their remembering. In this moment, I imagine us as mothers—two women made-for-tv-whole and smiling.

I've been brainstorming steps to transform us. We've been asked to rate heartbreak—a lover's back pierced and blooming center mass. Strange how often I've been told the heart is female—how it homes feelings. All our heart wants is to pump and pump, locked tight in his warm cage of muscle and bone.

The first time I loved, at the end she punched my face, held me against a wall by my throat. I want to tell you this memory makes me feel like a fish. How I wished in that moment to be slick and blue. How I wish for it still. Here you aren't female but an octopus or jelly. And we can both forget how my right breast still drips milk for our daughter in a hot shower.

Once, after a surgery, I asked you for my journal. In my hospital bed—high on morphine, drain tubes stitched into my belly—the pages filled and filled. Weeks later, I sat down at my desk to type. Every page was blank.

I can't casually discuss what is coming for me. Our marriage won't survive you explaining long term care insurance again. Today, in your group: a cousin in diapers, paralyzed child, incoherent texts from a sister in an assisted living facility, blind mother of six. Tonight, I will kiss our sleeping children in their beds. One last kiss before I turn off the living room lights and walk across the house to our bedroom. I'll brush my teeth. I'll undress. I'll climb into our bed.

Blackest Black

I confirm I am not Anish Kapoor.

As one does, sew the lids, glue lips, clench and clench
and clench, and leave this place behind, rearview mirror

shadow collapsing into shadow—this blackest black
wasn't meant for us. But even we, we lift our arms,

fall—elegant as the chosen feathered fallen. Even we,
as some do, travel on down roads blackening in the paint-dark night.

Pain as Memoir

Like winter paints strokes of naked birch across a canvas washed with watered pigment—the between blue and leaden green of your eyes—I've painted a memoir of gray. I know I took too long to say plainly how often my silence meant I was dreaming of running, too often I imagined stopping the car, disappearing into the nearest field. Like winter, I never cared much if someone found me—or when—if I'd be flesh, or if my skin would have feathered and blown to the ground as leaves to crumble and dance in January frost. Only the children in the back of our van stopped me, their faces waiting. How their lips would have blued, their breath. Not you. And I'm sorry. You lost me to sadness. I should have told you pain had painted my eyes, sealed my mouth. I should have told you again and again, I no longer believe you love me.

I can't forget, can't return, all the once

purple-blues: teeth clamped on lip, blood
like hotsalt, tongue a fat steak, pain alivehungry,
and all the words I don't remember, *hungry*.
I can't forget *pain*. The mouth remembers

how pain sleeps, struggles, waits. The mouth
knows pain will come, has come, is coming,
this way comes through memory—white fade
before anesthesia—knows to wake

or not to wake. I don't always want to wake. Imagine
the last true truth you were sure of, that solid cold
solid glass marble swirling blueyellow in your palm,

is now just sand churning your legs in water.

Elegy for My Wife

You push your tongue into your bottom lip in concentration when you fuck me, furrow your eyebrows, fall on and further into me. That night you explained it all, you lay next to my just fucked body, my numb and burning legs. I'll always remember how we laughed.

Please remember all the pronouns, *you* and then *you* again, mean you and sometimes not you. Or sometimes both. All you smooth-bodied, you gliders and sure-footers, you walkers and passers and named—all you non-divergent—sometimes, I'm implicating. That is painful too. But we can all share that burn together when you fuck me.

Here I do mean requiem. I mean music and keening, but I won't wail for your dead name. I don't mean that violence. I wish for a word other than *elegy* to explain how some of this feels like goodbye. An editor once wrote in a rejection letter that my *elegy* was offensive. But it's true how these cold nights we use our fingers and tongues to say goodbye to the bodies we knew.

When you go—your body—when your smooth face is replaced by stubble and your voice deepens, I may think about the nights we held onto the wet of each other. I'm not crying loss. I want to tell you water falls blue and cleansing as childhood—summer hose, hint of rubber in the back of your throat. I'm not crying shame either, not for you anyway.

Some shame cloaks and dusts all of the body like water slicks stones. Some shrinks the body from the rocky tumble of stone slick stone against stone. We both understand shame.

I worry we will lose the night I pushed our daughter's body from my body, how later you held her bloody body to your naked chest. Shame is my fear of empty spaces left behind in me—small feet pressed running into yesterday's wet sand—and I'm filling that darkness with my crying.

This is an elegy for your breasts, your softness, and how your body pushed against my body was like pushing hard into a mirror.

Shame lives in our old crooks, the dark and dwelling recesses—spoon slapped from my small chubby hand, your long teenage-silence drives to your mother's church therapist, and all the other ways our bodies have failed us.

I'll hold tight to how—in birth—my body opened and opened, how my tongue pushed into my teeth, my lips blued from my held pushing breath, and how you filled the ache—with your fingers and tongue—that lingered so long after our release.

I see us all now, standing in the thick of it, life like sleeping bees in our hair.

II.

I strive to remain liquid.
—EULA BISS

This is the Only Conversation We Will Have About the Embryos

This week we spend the cold days on ocean overcast brown sand. You call it *gloomy*. But the weather reports the closest lightning strike is 176 miles away—no rain in our forecast. In another part of the country, baseball-sized hail and a child crushed in her bed by a fallen tree. The children wade. I sit wrapped in a yellow flannel blanket.

Husband, we've discussed pain beyond pain before. Imagine something delicate and beloved crumpled and balled into the garbage. Imagine walking away. Every woman who has lost is sitting here with me on this damp sand.

Husband, some mornings I try to convince myself to die just to feel the goodness of *certainty* in my chest—so warm and safe this act tricks my muscles.

We are seaside for the air—salt will seep through my skin to my nerves. Some strange alchemy of ocean and air will rebuild myelin in the gaps—neck, brain, spine. The whole family prays to the ocean. White-breasted birds call to each other, wobble too close to the children's toes. Vacation birds are all less ominous than the constant unkindness of Missouri ravens. Soft steps print their aimlessness in the hard sand.

Fly Season

Maggots rise each morning from driveway expansion joints. We tack fly strips in the pantry and windows. We pay the older children a quarter for every kill. My husband buys a pressure washer—standard suburban starter kit: minivan, privacy fence, sectional sofa. Still maggots rise each morning to die on the double car driveway.

Wild garlic takes over the front bed. We pull and pull and pull. The cat uses the vegetable garden as a litter box. Our son keeps a tomato spider as a pet, collects grasshoppers from the unmowed grass, pulls off legs and chucks bodies into webbing. Basil in the window box has flowered. Their political signs go up and up in every neighboring yard. We are surrounded.

Last year, two men a few miles over had their car vandalized twice. *Faggots* in red paint on the hood and doors. The police came. *Don't worry.* Their three children weren't home when the house burned to the ground. Lighter fluid. Last month, two women a town over—gasoline—were asleep with their son in their bed. Our son collected his old toys into plastic grocery bags. We brought a casserole to the extended stay—yes, in these parts, we do all know each other.

Mike waves. Clarence too. Megan and Dave have us over for dinner. We can only walk half our block anyway before my legs give out, before I need the cane. We keep mostly to our high-fenced back yard. Flies sneak in the back door, the hole in our kitchen window screen on my husband's to-do list. Flies swarm our legs. Flies catch in my hair, buzz and buzz and buzz.

Pain as Caged Birds

My husband is leaving behind his body captor. I am every day entering the body that will cage me. Cage me in the memory of a body without pain. I'm jealous of his healing. I am slowing—transparent film placed over the same still frame. I'm paused, fading to pink. It is difficult for others to see how we will never be what we were, and I will never be what I would have been. Film too close to a melting light.

I am in a pit looking up at you all backlit above. I want to ask if you think of oceans, as I do—in bed, in the shower, over ham and potatoes at dinner. I want to write each moment as trauma, imagine that is all that I am. I am in love with despair, mine a lovely blue-green-eyed hauntling, sweet-smiled, clean and helpful.

There are women who will tell you they are blessed: *A woman can learn a truth inside the center of pain.* How to live the fable of floaters crisscross-legged from their mats, those who silence for years in burned-incense air, those who humble live and live gratitude. You imagine we enlightened women know something you don't. We truth tellers. We fable makers. But nothing can be learned from pain except what it is to feel pain.

I know why so many of the sick and dying worship gratitude. My cells die and replace themselves—five days, fourteen days, fifteen years—I am partially new and yet . . . still always dying.

I remember fall days on a blanket pressing leaves with crayons into thin paper, finger paint prints, acorns. I'm naked now, printing my body to a mattress; I'm too burning for clothes. Some afternoons I drift to sleep between the drugs. As I fall, I imagine death is like this—warm. I tell my therapist the antidepressants are killing me. I can't cry or connect a color to the feeling of my son's hand in mine. I can't find a word for how this warm sleep tastes. *Interesting*, she says.

I'm finally finding anger—small and burning. This anger reminds me of those first nights at nine or ten when I thought just right about that girl on TV—squeezed my thighs tight, laid on my belly. This too was pain—glands flexing and squeezing for the first time. How the only solution then was to rub the pain away.

Cry out with me.

Does it feel strange on your feet? The technician asks. *I can't feel my feet*, I reply as we side-step side-step in the underwater treadmill—strange slow dancers without music. We could almost be mistaken for lovers nearly in love if a camera would swirl around us. We stand face-to-face, hold hands gently over the water. The audience dizzies from the spinning. I imagine some film school professor once associated vertigo with love and now here we are.

I can't explain the difference between rising and falling: breasts and lungs, the lurch of intestines shuffling, scrambling to find their seats again. Every movie has taught me the end matters more than the journey. I can't make sense of it. I'm comforted that you'll all be this dead one day, too.

I'm watching my husband give himself his weekly shot. The spouses in my online group are so angry. They say: *This isn't what I signed up for.* I'm angry too. His lovely body is becoming whole. My body has become a shell. I pretend each day to be what I'm not. I tell my therapist some people's lives seem never to spin so wildly out of control. She says, *It can seem like that.* Sometimes I want to ask her, *Can you hear the strange fire singing?*

Daughter, before you thought in words

did you think the sound of my singing, green of my eyes, give of my breasts, scratch of my pen? Did you see yourself in the glow of sunned snow-light from your bedroom window? Every room in our house is glowing and we are glowing. Today you are older, toothed and walking. I am older too. Your face spots pink when you scream. I see how anger spreads across your forehead, down your ears as a fever. I've lost so much time trying to burn the smell of you into me: wood and light like the sliver under my childhood door. Some part of me survives in your neck and mouth and ears. I press into you again and again. My only thought the celebration of our coming together and pulling apart.

3 am on the toilet, the shell forgets

to piss, falls asleep, wakes and tries to try to remember what happens on the toilet and how and why. The shell forgets to worry when it wakes on the toilet at 3 am. This is disorienting later, to remember how it felt to sit without worry.

The shell on the toilet in the silent house hasn't forgotten the year, just history and aging and all that pressed on the synapses. One foot on the tile and another in an ocean—barely rolling water, black and reflective. Then the shell pisses. Wakes and pisses some more. And sleeps again. Wakes. None of it is normal. I should tell someone.

The piss—in spurts and stops like a teenager learning stick on the neighborhood hill because that is the only way—is comforting. The shell remembers learning and a father patient on the truck bench, but many other somethings are missing: black mechanical plastic, slurps against skin and a curling, pulling tongue, satisfaction at a button diagonaling into a too tight slit for the first time. Then some more piss.

The shell forgets children are in the house and how many, occasionally remembers children exist—how skin softly hardens at the heels and elbows, the first crunch of cinnamoned sugar on toast in the mouth, jumping bones that bend and run on landing—is startled by how fortunate it is for them to be so helpless and goes back to sleeping or pissing.

The shell writes sections of poems I don't remember in the morning. Brilliant work. I should tell my therapist. I suspect this is dementia—only the shell and pissing is so pleasant I'd rather not stop. Pleasant is the wrong word. The word is an adjective that means I'm a girl still living in the past and future and good at baking and puzzles and nude. The shell and forgetting at 3 am on the toilet, sleeping and waking and pissing and sleeping are the best part of my day.

I know I'm still breathing from my lungs

because breath spills like pollen emptied
into a summer wind sweet with sun and buzzing
traffic—lights halt and go and flash—still breathing
as children swim the neighborhood pond lost
shoes in the drain running grass
blades wings pulled luminescent
night flashed moon like a tom peeking
the peep and chirp and laughter—breathing still—
and waiting the wait
for the creep of blackblack
turning my breath breathless
as leaves and redorange fall whispers.

Let's stay here with the geese and strays
the warm wet knee pit and sweet
musk under our clothes
safesafe here and home together.

Running as Self-Portrait

Movie women run horror-mouthed and tousled—we're trained to see this as beautiful—through fields of corn, tall fall grasses, unclassifiable foliage green and thick and swelling with anticipation. Directionless women—the running is significant. We imagine how it must feel on their naked faces—needles crown leaves, wisp and zip along all the women have exposed. Running.

I'm the running, not the before or after. We believers, we followers, we kneelers at the temple of neurons traveling. We who worship at the feet of pain have been cured of before and after.

Sometimes a child is running—barefoot and good—someone or something beloved tearing behind them through the dust and green. Sometimes laughter. Sometimes foot sunk sloshed mud sprays on calves. We imagine deepened freckles and sun skin smell. Running.

We know in the running both running stories are true and both are lie like the word *unconditional*—how it tingles in the mouth of a lover uttering in the sweating blanketed darkness.

Everyone Waits at the DMV

Breath, cottony and damp, poured into your mouth
from another mouth. Lowing strings fill silences.
This sound must be a cello. On a road not empty,
not dark or untread, every passerby is a stranger,
all the lights red and blinking. A floor so glossy

it doesn't seem to touch any feet but reflects:
a poster, a clock, a chair. Some may feel their bodies
reverse. So we are. A white-haired caterpillar on the back
of a hand wades the hairs like flood water.
Leaves turn orange and burn too early or too late

and our memory of exactly when somehow always lost.
A child dies. So we are. Unvoiced conversations
spoken through the widening and narrowing
whites of eyes across a room. Fly in the house.
Ants on the baseboard. Water, cold and weeping,

walked to the sofa by a lover or mother. Suspect
on the loose. Close the windows. A chill in our guts.
So we are. Endings are like lowering your own body
onto something wet and crumbling. Loving, the good bits,
is like frantic scrambling for something you've misplaced.

Cataloguing Pain as Non-Narcotic Pain Reliever

My children beg to be loved with cartwheels and screams. I read once about microchimeric cells, know I still carry the children inside me. My mother lives in me too—a silent, slow swimmer. I know I'll still belong to them when I can't remember how I shit as I pushed my children from my body.

I'm wearing my old maternity clothes around the house. *So brave*, they'll say at my funeral. If I can do this well—this slow death from disease and medication—I'll finally be lovable. My therapist calls this a martyr complex. *Someone must witness the chrysalis, the knife, how it burns to expand and dry and shake in the shell*, I tell her. *Interesting*, she says.

My face has aged and tired, so I open my eyeshadow palette. Pigment dust poofs into the white subway tile bathroom. The smell reminds me of my mother. I can love the eye bags darkened even more by the overhead light and leave well enough alone.

In the sun-shadowed yard, my baby's fingers brush and splash in the grass. She speaks mostly gibberish now. My husband reads the newspaper. The older children read on swings. I think I'm writing a love letter to them, to us, to the words we fit together, to my body turning slowly to floating light.

I hold hands with my son on our sofa. My daughter brings ice packs. The whole family holds me after a fall—you might not see it, but this is beautiful. We teach our children to dial 911. They memorize our address. They will understand how to give to another body in need of a body pressed tight to the skin.

A new specialist asks if I take any medications. I laugh, hand her a list a page long, remember when my answer was *multivitamin*. After the exam, the doctor and nurse huddle behind a computer to find a medicine that won't kill me, settle on one with the side effect of making my Xanax stronger. *I'll take it!* I try to act concerned, serious.

Our baby's scream flies into our bed at five in the morning. I don't wake enough to hold her, change her diaper. She settles into the nacre of our bodies spooned face to face and knee to knee. In a fog, I move to adjust blankets and my husband's hand grabs mine in the dark. Rough. Warm. He covers me in the dark.

Some nights our bodies still bend into negative space left to fill by our curving flesh. Our bodies whisper vows again and again—your mouth on my ear like our first drenched *I love you.* I want you inside me, your hand on mine.

Each of my children fed from my breasts, wrapped their tight hands tight around my index finger as they tippled and dozed on my belly. This is the tight I feel. Not the electric pain of information pulsing over batter nerves, pain that bands my legs and chest—the memory of my children squeezes me.

I like to use both feet to cover our standing shower's drain—watch the fiberglass basin fill and fill. I imagine water filling our bathroom. This water is beautiful and safe as blue sunlight. My husband and children swim with me, strange aquatic mammals.

Acknowledgments

Many thanks to the editors of the following magazines for publishing several of the poems included here, sometimes in earlier forms:

Anti-Heroin Chic: "Pain as Memoir" originally published as "Memoir of Gray"
ellipsis . . . literature & art: "Daughter, before you thought in words"
Fatal Flaw: "A Catalogue of Repetitive Behaviors"
Foglifter: "Fly Season"
Grub Street Literary Magazine: "Pain as Caged Bird"
Mayday Magazine: "How To Be Gay In Missouri"
Mom Egg Review: "The Name in the Doorway"
Orange Blossom Review: "Cataloguing Pain as Marriage Counseling"
Raleigh Review: "Cataloguing Pain as Non-Narcotic Pain Reliever"
Sinister Wisdom: "How To Be Gay In Missouri"
SWWIM Every Day: "Fall Risk" and "During the Days After my Official MS Diagnosis"
the museum of americana: "Everyone Waits at the DMV"
Toad The Journal: "On a good night, we feel like talking. In our bed, I explain to my wife" (Originally published as "The Supreme Court Hears Oral Arguments Against Gay Marriage")
West Trestle Review: "A Poem for When You Ask What's Wrong."

Several of the poems in this book were included in the chapbook *Susurration* (Blue Lyra Press, 2019).

This book is dedicated to my husband, my partner, my favorite person. Taylor, if I ever lose all of my words, know we made something beautiful together. I'm grateful we learned to grow with each other. I'm grateful you lived through these moments with me. You are, as always, the ground where I land and the air holding me together.

I am sincerely grateful for the help and encouragement of many writers and editors:

I'm incredibly lucky to have worked with the faculty at Queens. Thank you Sally Keith, Claudia Rankine, Morri Creech, Alan Michael Parker, and Jon Pineda.

Thank you Lynn Melnick for answering questions and supporting my work. Thank you Anna Leahy for your support and constant generosity.

Thank you Josh Davis, Joan Kwon Glass, Michelle Hendrixson Miller, Richard Allen Taylor, Greg Stapp, Julie Ramon, Roland Sodowsky, Chris Anderson, Melissa Fite Johnson, Lori Martin, and Shuly Cawood for reading, editing, and encouraging.

Thank you Laura Lee Washburn for being my mentor, teacher, and friend. I am deeply indebted to you and your students who let me crash workshop.

Thank you to the amazing staff at *Literary Mama* and *the museum of americana* and for the support of MSTU Write.

Thank you to my Small Harbor family—the staff and authors I've been so lucky to work with—Sarah Freligh, July Westhale, Anna Leahy, Dustin Brookshire, Carole Symer, Arden Levine, Joan Kwon Glass, Boston Gordon, Darren C. Demaree, Kristin LaFollette, Shareen K. Murayama, Kimberly Ann Priest, Sarah Rose Nordgren, Hannah Martin, Callista Buchen, Claire Eder, and Kristiane Weeks-Rogers.

Thank you Allison Carter for always telling me we will get through it together.

I'm grateful to Karen Kilgariff and Georgia Hardstark for the podcast *My Favorite Murder*. This book is the email I never sent to you. My husband introduced me to the podcast while I was paralyzed and recovering from a spinal tap. You've gotten us through so many hospital stays. Thank you for making us laugh through the rough parts.

Thank you to KMA Sullivan and all of the staff at YesYes Books. KMA, thank you for your keen editorial eye and generosity. You were a joy to work with. Publishing with YesYes has been my dream and goal since I began writing. I will always be grateful for the opportunity.

Also from YesYes Books

FICTION
Girls Like Me by Nina Packebush
Three Queerdos and a Baby by Nina Packebush

WRITING RESOURCES
Gathering Voices: Creating a Community-Based Poetry Workshop by Marty McConnell

FULL-LENGTH COLLECTIONS
Ugly Music by Diannely Antigua
Gutter by Lauren Brazeal
What Runs Over by Kayleb Rae Candrilli
This, Sisyphus by Brandon Courtney
40 WEEKS by Julia Kolchinsky Dasbach
Salt Body Shimmer by Aricka Foreman
Forever War by Kate Gaskin
Ceremony of Sand by Rodney Gomez
Undoll by Tanya Grae
Loudest When Startled by luna rae hall
Everything Breaking/For Good by Matt Hart
Sons of Achilles by Nabila Lovelace
Landscape with Sex and Violence by Lynn Melnick
Refusenik by Lynn Melnick

GOOD MORNING AMERICA I AM HUNGRY AND ON FIRE by jamie mortara
Stay by Tanya Olson
a falling knife has no handle by Emily O'Neill
To Love An Island by Ana Portnoy Brimmer
Another Way to Split Water by Alycia Pirmohamed
One God at a Time by Meghan Privitello
I'm So Fine: A List of Famous Men & What I Had On by Khadijah Queen
If the Future Is a Fetish by Sarah Sgro
Gilt by Raena Shirali
Say It Hurts by Lisa Summe
Boat Burned by Kelly Grace Thomas
Helen Or My Hunger by Gale Marie Thompson
As She Appears by Shelley Wong

RECENT CHAPBOOK COLLECTIONS

Vinyl 45s
- *Inside My Electric City* by Caylin Capra-Thomas
- *Exit Pastoral* by Aidan Forster
- *The Porch (As Sanctuary)* by Jae Nichelle
- *Juned* by Jenn Marie Nunes
- *Unmonstrous* by John Allen Taylor
- *Preparing the Body* by Norma Liliana Valdez
- *Giantess* by Emily Vizzo

Blue Note Editions
- *Kissing Caskets* by Mahogany L. Browne
- *One Above One Below: Positions & Lamentations* by Gala Mukomolova

www.ingramcontent.com/pod-product-compliance
Lightning Source LLC
Chambersburg PA
CBHW072011090426
42734CB00033B/2507